Luminous Bodies

ES CHARLTON

For Zoe,

Happy Birthday!

18/3/02

and love from

James

17 · 02 · 02

Luminous Bodies

JAMES CHARLTON

Published by
Montpelier Press
21 Pillinger Street
Dynnyrne Tasmania 7005
Australia

The publication of this book was assisted through Arts Tasmania by the Premier, Minister for State Development and The Regional Arts Fund, a Commonwealth Government initiative through the Australia Council, its arts funding and advisory body.

Cover painting by Luke Wagner, *Luminous Bodies, After the Poem by James Charlton*
Cover design by Lynda Warner
Photo of James Charlton by Noeline Robinson
Typesetting and design by ACYS Publishing
Printed by Terry Brophy & Assoc.

ISBN 1 876597 08 9

Acknowledgments

Poems in this collection have been previously published, sometimes in different forms, in the following magazines, newspapers or anthologies:
Along These Lines (ed. C.A. Cranston), *Bulletin*, *Canberra Times*, *Centoria*, *Effects Of Light* (eds. Vivian Smith and Margaret Scott), *Eremos*, *Famous Reporter*, *First Rights* (eds. Michael Denholm and Andrew Sant), *Hobo*, *The International Terminal* (a Mattara anthology, ed. Christopher Pollnitz), *Island*, *Mattoid*, *Moorilla Mosaic* (eds. Robyn Mathison and Lyn Reeves), *New England Review*, *No Strings Attached* (eds. Jeff Guess and Fiona Johnston), *Overland*, *Prairie Schooner*, *Quadrant*, *Republic Readings* (ed. Liz Winfield), *Studio*, *Sufi*, *Sunday Tasmanian*, *Tirra Lirra*, *Togatus*, *Two Centuries Of Australian Poetry* (2nd edition; ed. Mark O'Connor), *Ulitarra*, *Urthona*, *Vernacular*, and *Westerly*. Various poems have been read on ABC Radio National and on Radio 5UV.

I wish to thank Arts Tasmania and the Literature Fund of the Australia Council for invaluable support during the period when many of these poems were written.

Thanks, also, to Fiona Wilson for initial, vital encouragement; to our son Richard Charlton; and to Sonja Vanderaa, principal encourager and critic, to whom I dedicate this book.

Contents

1

Yellow-tailed Black Cockatoos

Random as rags whooshed off a truck,
        they indolently amble on the air. This caterwaul:
                wee-la. Yes, there,

husky, high. It seems an idle sortie,
        a lope of meander-flight, a frittering in the eye
                of foul weather.

Gale winds begin to split and peel
        a suburb of weather-board husks, but the flock
                keeps following its memory-grid

to grubs in weakened trees. (Birds like these
        saw dinosaurs plod through dust.)
                They prise, rip,

rasher the acacia bark, and change trees,
        wheeling and veering like black Venetian blinds
                collapsed at one end.

Then they dip, curious,
        to an English willow;
                shimmy down bare verticals on hinge-claws;

whir out
        on a glissade of whoops:
                concertina-tailed, splay-winged, wailing.

Absence

Your absence
holds the shape
of your face.

I repeat your name
in the night.

This chair
where you sat;
those days

in the park –
how far we wandered
in those days;

our manners delicate,
the air gentle.

A discontented man
would stare at you;

a burdened woman
look away
and feel

that she was you,
back when …
and one day, you'd be her.

Tasman Peninsula

Climbing a headland which faces a grey swathe
stretching to Antarctica,
    I walk the precipice rim
    to scan chasm edges
and see a petrel,
            bird of husky alto
            and straight drop dive

dive to a garfish. The petrel's beak points
to nothing except the fish, which in turn
symbolises nothing but itself,

            a lesson I resisted,
much as that raptor
resists plummeting to garfish,
    an easy talon-catch it wouldn't rise from,
    should the ragged up-curvings of its rust wings
    prove unequal to a wave's down-curling.

One afternoon, as the heat thrust upward,
I watched the wing-tip touchings of falcons courting,
their aerial spiral
        of tip touch,
    bank away,
            retouch.

    Always, an unfixed interplay,
    invisible with visible:
    turbulence, purple shadow, diverse currents.

I pause to greet momentary things,
nature's ebullient commerce.   A stick

transmutes into an insect; in the bay
where we learnt to swim, supported underneath
by arms gentling lowering our bodies on the swell,
a fish transmutes into a sponge.

Drawn, almost,
to pass beyond sense, reflective thought,
                            its structures, definitions,
I loop down to a marsupial lawn.
Casuarinas lean landwards from long habit,
raindrops pearling from their branches.

Small skulls move me,
                     of themselves,
but signify nothing beyond life, death.

I re-enter the shack
and feel I'm entering someone else's.
                     Losing sight of needs, desires,
                            I'm slightly different,
                            yet the same.

The fly which buzzes over a wombat,
killed on the highway;
an infant wombat, asleep in this pullover,

                            and the pullover itself;
                                   medicinal oil scent,
                                          thick fur's clamminess;

      heave of in breath
            and soft wheeze
                     of out breath:

specific material realities,

coherent in their origin and end:
wombat, casuarinas,
petrel, garfish, waves:

not the knowledge
that each belongs to all
and all to each,

but an immediate grasp,
an embrace of wide-armed uselessness,
as when you don't see a door ajar
and your face strikes it:
experience of the bruising world
and us
immersed in the unnameable
which imbues all praises and laments,
abides in all things,
ever united, ever distinct.

The distant waves dissolve,
re-shape,
dissolve,

barely cover
firmly rooted
lurching kelp.

Lesser Long-eared Bat

Crinkly and frail

as a fresh scab

on an old man's knuckle,

this tiny bat

which flew in the door

and flitted over the candle-lit room

has hung her cape of curled suede

on the hat rack.

Turning the crushed violet

of her head

to face me,

she eyes me close up

from very far away.

Tinderbox Hills

In the headache of an afternoon
a grapefruit speaks about roundedness in life,
pungency; a pale stalk

retiring into a paler ring. A warm breeze
whispers the piquancy of herbs.
Bracken roots, like monkeys' fingers,

loop along the edges of our garden.
Eucalyptus-raffia dangles
over the bracken's spatter work,

while underneath, jack-jumper ants
remodel their civic centres.
Erratic weather:

we wake to the eucalypts' sway and whirl.
A disc of woven twigs – a heron's nest –
spins to the ground, killing both chicks.

Their mother reappears the next calm afternoon.
She kneels by a water bowl,
levers herself sideways,

and then, composed in height,
vibrates a foot on a bed of alyssum
to flush out moths.

A neighbour drives up.
There's talk of certain bees
which carry tiny pebbles to avoid being blown off course.

This Rabbit

You feel like shooting this rabbit
among the seedlings,
except you ponder
how he squats within one mind,
tastes the seedlings
in nonconceptual flavours,
accepts his experience
for what it is.

Parsnip, broccoli, spinach.

His pale feet shudder.

One pulse ceases;
another quickens.
One set of teeth jerks open;
another clenches.

On the Rim
(for Michael Tate)

In the present dark,
our bodies, these portable monasteries,
sit on the rim of silence.
Brought here by someone's touch,
our narrowing attention
enters the practice of stillness.

Perhaps a teacher with the spirit's
fullness,
or a disinterested friend
(the family dog, say)
touched us from a quiet place
of infinite expansion.

It could have been friends
less concerned
with what they can control
than with openness
to living the mystery.
Likely as not, they still cavort somewhere,

holding together opposites,
willing to commit themselves to outcomes
of which they can have
no inkling,
pleased to bear
the unexplained, the vague,

happy to say *don't know*
to something vital
and not feel ignorant,

or, not knowing what to do,
    remain present (say)
to another who needs presence ...

    Touched, somewhere,
by one such being
    with tinctures of this recognition,
we began to be still,
    began to see:

    all that matters is embodiment,
these envelopes of sense and soul.
    To be faithful to the vision,
to the action.
    All that matters
is the experience of communion,

    unspeakable communion
in the silent depths.
    Here is our surrender, beyond all seeking.
Here, the inexhaustible meaning.
    It is not separate from the vision,
from the action. Not separate from This.

Bird Studies

Curled lip of bird-bath
worn thin with claw-cuts.
Hot evenings: a knit-a-thon
of single needles. Wattlebirds
lower the water
for lesser honeyeaters, easing
their click and cast-off.
Fledgelings shuffle
in a queue. A wagtail
crochets the air.

*

A gust of starlings
waddles the lawn.
An umbrella opens in a hurry.

*

Pardalotes in a eucalypt:
swatches of brocade.
A kookaburra, in flak jacket
with baseball cap, swoops to unpick stitches.

*

In the mangrove
  that mocks the sea,
      a black-necked stork
for personal reasons
    claps her bill.

Perhaps the paw-paw sunset calls: *Clap now!*
                    or distant semaphore of wing beat
                                        finds reply.

*

A blue wren hops sideways on a sill
to strike his own reflection with his feet.
Four weeks elapse: his feet are baggy-white with pus.

*

Nesting plovers screech at the lamb,
not knowing their eggs
are already trampled.

*

Dazed honeyeater squats
on grandma's palm,
tilts its head as if
assessing her.

Life's no longer
further on,
or next,
but now
and slow
and cradled
in a choice
to either stay
or go.

A Lagavulin Night

A friend of ours is dead,
and yet confronts us when

we toss in bed.
Anything positive, we ask,

to shatter our projections?
Yes, she says, *I'm with the One*

to whom all creatures come,
if they care to.

Any more reality, we ask,
to ease the treachery of theory?

Yes, she says,
I'm in a country you've already

entered; in a house
you've already seen.

Each Needle Fuming

We walk into night drizzle; moonlight trellises ferns and orchids anchored high in the canopy. Our spotlight drifts across basket and bird's-nest ferns, the largest hanging like rucksacks from tree sides. Around us, aerial roots form a massive screen. Fig greenery consorts in the canopy with the tops of subordinate trees. The whole weave comprises a suspended world, steadied like a huge marquee by cables of fig. This is jungle's mid-way zone, not high enough for permanent twilight and mist.

Meandering through lianas and lawyer vines, you trip on a root, fall into a thicket of stinging trees. Tiny silica hairs dislodge from heart shaped leaves, both sides. Onslaught, poison-spurt. Convulsion of face, neck and arms. Hot undulations: each embedded needle fuming in its site. Mareeba hospital: sticking plaster is laid across your skin, section by section, then peeled away. In greenish light, you drift – my love – toward sedated sleep.

Koonya
Cape Barren Island, 1828

She wore a sheen of possum fat,
ran from the surf with high-up knees,
kept orange starfish in a pool.
She flayed the sky with kelp straps,
jumped out giggling from behind rocks

until caught by the heels
and tied below deck.
They fed her in the sealers' hut,
changing the leash after each month's work.
She coughed up oyster pulp,

and those white barnacles she grew
inflamed Dan Smith with their rasp.
He buttoned his trousers,
trussed up her legs,
took her out the back,

fired a flintlock in her ribs.
There in the Cape Barren dunes,
under midden shells,
her chipped nails claw
the evasive sand.

High Country, behind Hobart

The brow of The Mountain has wrinkled
and shed a slope of plinths.
Hikers see them as giant thumbs
thrust through mossy clefts,
tilted in tiredness.

Ice invades a crack,
demands a fissure,
undoes the dolerite –
as any form of water might abrade
the harder facts of history.

Snow-melt prattles down
to a city's foetid river.
On the farthest shore,
green hills are topped
with jaggedy grey,

as if tufted dirty wool
in a wet rug is being teased,
this way and that. Above this: froth,
peaky as whipped egg white. The hills unravel
in skeins of vapour; a streak of murk coaxes up a squall.

To Governor George Arthur in Heaven

You didn't fornicate, swear or drink.
You didn't cheat or hate.
Each night, studying Scripture,
you thanked the Lord for dying to save you.
In the mornings you dangled the guilty.
Their throats were tightened after prayers,
and "all but the most insensible
showed signs of repentance."

I should not judge –
you did not choose your code.
But talk with Mary MacLauchlan,
dragged from husband and family in Glasgow;
transported for theft to Van Diemen's Land.

Remember stretching her for infanticide,
8 a.m., Monday, April the 19th, 1830?
At least you couldn't sleep –
struggled with that verse about yea be yea
and nay nay – and shunned the leading citizen
who seduced her.

Ask Mary about that final letter
to two small daughters,
and life's last walk, on air.

Hobart 4 pm, mid-winter

Where Lieutenant Hunter disembarked,
the shore now foams with industrial outwash.
Rainbowed water rims pebbles.

In the distance, a corner of the river's mouth
grips the Iron Pot Lighthouse, which clocks on,
as we watch, to lick the ocean.

On waving slopes of weeds, plovers fuss over precedence,
like Freemasons. Lieutenant Hunter brought thistle seed
in a reliquary; supervised the landing of a satchel
of dandelion fluff.

Perhaps he also brought blackberry seeds, baskets
of starlings, blackbirds and sparrows. Rabbits, maybe,
in wickerwork crates. Tucked up with his luggage,
sweet briar cuttings and canisters of gorse.

Scrub once grew close to the river's edge;
children once played in the dunes.

Convict Brick

A pile of broken bricks
protruding from the bracken
near the beach.

Koonya outpost –
where British redcoats
had their barracks built
by a herd of convicts.

This brick –
its well-known glow
of reddish warmth, riper apricot;
its intimate indentation.

What other imprint
could a prisoner make?
What other way
to penetrate space
with sense?

Truganini's Soliloquy

I have known Earth's texture
like another skin.
All my life I have seen
the unseen entities. Each one
reflects a light beyond colour,
a light which paints
all colour into being.

When I was young, a white man
came to my shelter.
He'd heard the night-chorus,
but complained he couldn't sleep,
having failed to hear the song behind the noise.
And when the new-created light
quivered through the slattings,
and shoals of eucalypt leaves
waved their shadows over us,
he wanted blinds, curtains.

I think he only saw Earth's foreground –
his eyes roving for quarry.

The white men broke our circle,
which stretched outwards, like the sky's vastness.
Their leaders thought we needed to be overseen.
If I'd known their words, I would've said:

You have lost the all-embracing song
which nurtures the past
into the future. You have failed
to see the All-Encompasser:
One who inhabits the wind,

without being it; One who dwells
within the cutting grass, but isn't botanical.

The overseeing continues.
Pink heath is burnt; blackwoods cut down.
This is how the white man makes a garden.
Someone has planted 'hydrangeas'
in front of where I live,
saying: 'If the sun gets hot,
please cover them with an old sack.'

2

Luminous Bodies

Her old VW
mows the dirt road
to my shack,

past the noiseless fall
of frangipani,
a flash of butterfly

in deep shade.
We walk in the garden
of now,

and find an alcove
of tenderness
behind the melaleuca.

She listens
to the hidden life:
roots drawing nourishment,

sap rising in stems.
Each twig,
an inverse tongue;

each leaf and flower
a wisdom far removed
from knowledgeable din.

Infrangible desire:
a thousand cicadas
throbbing the heat.

Shyly assertive,
she sings my body;
I, hers.

We sing
the joy
of imperfection,

the caress
of impermanence.
Soft tissue,

exquisitely bruised,
collapses
into limb-sized folds.

One Light, Many Lamps

Caught short

by nightfall

in a forest;

chancing upon fungi,

luminescent.

Intense bluish-

white shards

would in the morning

be as cold as

crockery.

Peaked strata,

suspended

like tiers

of cave-homes

in Cappadocia,

where in silence

a countenance

was seen

and known,

and known to be

seeing back.

Just so,

the wilderness

sees those

who see it

on a late summer

night with stars,

a night to be brought

to sense

by sight

of the earthly.

This fungi:

a hardening

of light.

Beyond its bluish

glow, tiny beings

call their

complement.

Each of them,

a lamp;

each lamp

the embodiment

of one light.

To Your Fully Open Eyes

You have emerged from water
for a dot of time.
Your middle name is Pagan
– dweller in nature –
a slight exaggeration, since,
like any urbanite,
you check your hair
and double-check it looks alright.
You are evolution's intuition;
a sliver of light
not bound by clothes
or skin.
You hold exploding stars
and dust which weeps.

Only yesterday, it seems,
you stretched across me –
hands upon hands,
eyes upon eyes,
mouth upon mouth.
Confluent passions,
woven in the fabric of the deep,
will reach a oneness
beyond all purpose.

And so I praise your fully
open eyes,
the way they dwell alongside
your thoughts;
the way they live suspended happily
between hope and

hopelessness, beaming your portion
of time
into infinity's heart.
I praise these eyes which neither cling
nor push away,
but exalt in dappled light,
entertaining no wish
for life to be otherwise,
knowing themselves inseparable
from the evanescent,
like a banksia's fragrance,
briefly held
upon the motion of clean air,
after rain.

Creatures

These perfect, inverse cones:
tapped overnight in the soil
by a bandicoot's snout.

*

Falling from the sky: mutton birds.
Too fat to stay airborne
for Alaska, they crash onto the roof.

*

An echidna,
in need of water, waddles round
and round an unreachable bird bath.

*

Bronze as an antique bed-warmer,
the stag beetle whirs into a somersault,
slams against a gum tree
jerking the barbs on its fish-hook legs.

Grappling through December's sticky flowers
it twists on the edge of a leaf,
claws upward to the black-tipped spike
of a butcher-bird's beak.

*

Nothing unexpected
has happened;

just a potoroo,
hopping
to a verdant corridor,
fallen
on the road.
There is silence
in the scrub,
an absence
of paws holding roots,
an emptiness
among the wounded trees.

*

A woodlouse,
stretching its ovaline slate-plates,
climbs an apple tree to find a codling-hole.

On a Day of Still Heat

In the still heat
	a breadfruit ripens:
a multitude of tiny sunspots
	mounted on hexagonal platelets,
green leather skin
	and flesh of kneadable custard.

In the breadfruit
	is hidden the sun;
in the sun
	the breadfruit.
Before the heat reaches Earth,
	the flames have already died;
before being picked,
	the breadfruit is already rotten.

And all the unpurchaseable luxuries
	– beetles, thunder, pebbles, twigs –
whose lives say, simply,
	I *accept*,
are hidden in each other
	and hide all things.

After the Fire

The sought-for elder sat
on a flurry of tarpaulin,
his torso thinly rippled,
like a goanna's neck.

Laconically inclined,
he conveyed a sense
of humble self,
as if in-

capable
of charming ways
or being charmed.
Before him,

we sat cross-legged
and received the wind,
its texture of bush fire grit.

New shoots appeared beside a grey
talcum path; maggots
hatched into flies.

Down in a creek bed with curled
clay leaves,
we opened a basket of fruitfulness:
bread, berries, watermelon.

Our squinting eyes
resembled large ants;
our creased feet rested
like surplus loaves.

Susannah

your eyes, the colour
of an old brass tap,
match our scattered hats, your thick
weave of sun-glistened hair.

We slither off the diving plank
at Byron's pool,
to paint a wriggly fresco
on the water's skin.

    Further along the river bank,
    three fishermen hide under green umbrellas,
    propped in front of squat white cottages.

Kiss me again, Susannah,
behind the cherry orchard,
where wasps gyrate among
intimidated tourists.

Crush me, Susannah,
behind the hedgerow,
crush the tall dry grass
where no-one goes.

Billy Ah Foo

Derby, Tasmania, 1923

Against chills which wrack
his wood-splitting wrists
he eats a slice of cold fat
and drinks mutton-bird oil
from a spiral bottle.

Linseed-smelling home-made tools
pack his outside laundry. A watering can
gives shelter to a rainforest frog,
as common in the shire, then,
as an Edison cylinder.

The frog replies to Billy's simulated
croak, his bleak rendition of the one,
the lonely syllable. Bennett's wallabies
pressure the house-paddock's fencing.

A baggy tweed covers Billy's head,
shades a face softly leathered
like an early flying cap. From the verandah,
he might see the shapes of wallabies,
which lever their bodies closer

to the house, drawn by a slow folding
of human legs and arms. And if, by dint
of cataracts or deafness, Billy doesn't
see the wallabies or hear the frog, but simply
sits in shade, he could be light sitting in light.

Wedge-tail

Floats an eagle
        on an early evening's swirl,
                on a surge of January heat,

drawn upwards
        from creek plain stubble.
                Ragged, she fringes

the Western Tiers' sheerness,
        glances off rock,
                rises without wing beat. Seeking

a coolness at cloud base,
        her body settles on air,
                easefully recollected.

Beneath, the trees' bleached sinews
        cling to fissured rock. In one cleft,
                melded with entangled eucalypt,

is the wedge-tail's heaped stickwork, lined
        with layers of freshly torn,
                germicidal leaves.

Farm soil thins
        to a stone scattering.
                Myrtles still grow, tenuous,

confined to paddock margins, cliffs.
        Squinting, I watch the sky
                diminish her,

and think of armies co-opting grace
    and strength,
        hoisting their eagle icons.

The Awesome Benefits of Idleness

There was no schedule, no map –
just the sloughed skin of a snake,
tightened by wind,
between twigs. No itinerary, no plan;
just the stretched resonance
of a skin which seemed to hum
the simplest, deepest sound.
We camped where people walked
the edge of the conceivable –
a life exchanged in living mediums –
two thousand generations. In galleries
of corridor and crypt
we sensed a tribe connected elsewhere
than the ego. Simply to walk there,
a dislocation of our comfort;
we hoped to feel life's source and consummation.
On the river
a dragonfly alighted on the ridge
of a crocodile's fearnought eyelid.
Such power to wrench apart,
or tenderly hold hatchlings
in the cradle of her teeth.
We watched her tread
the underside of overhangs
in watershed escarpments,
and lope –
tar-spotted, duco-faded –
to billabongs. She skirted litterings
of rock
and thrashed across floodplains.

She is a totem
of universal balanced turbulence,
thrusting within a union
of action, being.

Cousin Gwen

Our cousin once declined
to be a body: not that she lived solely
in her mind: she saw and felt
everyday epiphanies –
    noughts and crosses on rabbits' noses;
    fire bursting banksia pods,
    dispersing seeds.

Like us,
she spent her life
switching back
and forth between
nailing Christ
to the cross (adding her own
wilfully ignorant nails)
and being nailed
there herself.

Lonely, she slept
behind stockades of epithets,
unaware
that questions
brought to closure remain
unanswered.

At forty,
Gwen felt cheated.
But a text appeared
upon a biscuit plate:
The former things
have passed away!
Look!

I make all things new!
It was as if
a finger poked her nerves,
straightened a kink,
or eased threads
in her cord of humanity.

Did she see
that she was not
so much a body
with a soul,
as a carnal word,
particular
yet undefined,
in the language
of mystery?
See, also,
that she had always
known this?

Mangrove Swamp

Mudskippers splatter their bodies
onto mud banks,
flash dorsal fins,
breathe from water-filled gill chambers.

Pairs of fiddler crabs bolt into holes.
Males wave their claws;
the females have caught on.

From mud, root shoots protrude
like nails, serve as stilts,
or thrust in and out.

At night, bats,
contorted as burnt match boxes,
frot mangrove pollen to set seeds.

Stroked by parental shadows,
young plants snorkel in brine.
Silt becomes mud
becomes land …

the whole swamp veined like a womb,
heaving and sighing;
heaving with a sucking sound
and a sigh.

For Anthony's Dog Cherokee

Life has evolved from shattered stars.
My left brain ruminates: how small we are.
My right brain's sold on visiting Mars.

Stellar dust begat our ancestors,
moulded underground in Zanzibar.
Life has evolved from shattered stars

which spun the elements on their arses,
turning the Bollinger to vinegar.
My right brain's sold on visiting Mars

in order to pick some magic flowers
for smoking in a Martian bar.
Life has evolved from shattered stars.

I will sit and contemplate the sutras,
feed you buffalo steak and sell the car.
My right brain's sold on visiting Mars.

A dog will escort you! was Zoroaster's
quip. He thought male arrogance bizarre.
Life has evolved from shattered stars.
My right brain's sold on visiting Mars.

St Kilda Beach

Far out from the clammy city
the coastal verge remains voluptuous:
scented breezes, hazy skies,

states of undress. A cat sways by
on pendulous legs; creepers straggle
over wooden frames.

A walk-through rosemary clump
and a beach of hot sand; an urge
to explore, but a feeling of torpor.

This shuttered guest house is cool, subdued;
its small mats scattered like after-thoughts
on floors of grey-black marble.

An aspidistra has latticed with roots
an ancient pot. Now and then, a silhouette
of the woman I desire.

Come, come. Go, go.

This glance
charged with
direct desire,
intensity:
this impulse
      – embracing,
            embraceable –
is also tender
possibly,
without calculation.

Eyes of oneness ask:
are you my face of faces?
From a body of oneness
      – depths,
            shallows –
they ask: *are you my true lover*
at last, and
at the last ?

Possum

1. Green Ringtail

The green ringtail, a Far North curio,
sleeps exposed on a branch,
almost Dodo in its waiting to be done in.

Even its diet involves danger:
leaves which, if you touch them,
inject agony.

Down at the resort, life is all jet-ski
or desultory. No-one has heard
of the green possum, though in dull weather
it feeds by day, and at night
the red eyeshine doesn't waver.

Short-muzzled, meek,
vociferously mute, it poses questions
and replies with nothing beyond necessity,
out on a limb.

2. Brushtails

Guttural wheezes
and the scour-scream
of old kitchens.
Hushed, staring over their shoulders,
they reflect torch glare
with eyes quizzical and cautious.
Blunt warriors;
bane of rose-fanciers
in fringe suburbs.

Protected, yet shot,
and shot twice more,
they plummet to earth, tails grasping.

3. Common Ringtail

Almost biddable in white vests, undulating
along laterals, singing antiphons
of unoiled hinge, a tambourine's leaf-shake.

Calm eucalypt air has drawn ringtails
from their nest to cross the bitumen to our trees.
We watch with qualms
a pair hesitate, then waddle toward us

holding their tails parallel to the road,
slightly rotating the tips.
The female laps water from a lid;

we stroke her tendril-tail, relish the prehensile
grip, complain about tree-felling to the male.
His tweeky voice might be an echo
of a far-off, toppling tree.

Father Kolbe

First, he learnt
the ascetic's daily art –
the slow givenness
of abnegation,

a way of dying
before death,
obedience
to life.

So that, years later
in Auschwitz,
when Commandant Fritsch
selects ten men
to die in reprisal
for one escape,
Kolbe offers himself
in place of prisoner #5659.

A guard watches
through a grille
as Kolbe leads the nine
in a drawn-out dance

until all die
except him,
and a suited man enters,
fumbles an injection, and leaves.

Kolbe looks at the lily.
The lily looks back.
He enters the Yes,
even as the Yes
has entered him.

3

Amy

Amy's feet smell of rose or lavender,
depending on which daughter has called in.
If, from a distance, her head resembles a salted plum,
her face, at closer range, reveals what she has valued.
A nurse says that Amy has no sense of reality,

but seems to pray all day, believing it's bedtime.
Others claim she is alert: the protrusion on her head,
like a parasitic plant, confirming the vigour of the host.
As a girl, they say, she would sit below the hill line,

and sketch desolate trees, the way they incised the air.
She would take a net of onion bag and wire,
and fail to catch a single butterfly.
Now, in the garden, she sits in silence
by the bougainvillea. A butterfly alights upon her lips.

Crushing Mint Leaves

To forgive your parents their minimal affections
on behalf of unselfconscious sacrifices;
to free your parents from failure's guilt

on behalf of their humanity –
here's where the ego melts,
or merely substitutes one sermonizing style
for another.

Ageing parents find grace
in gardens. Crushing mint leaves in an alcove,
or picking raspberries, they offer you
peculiar confessions. The trick is to remember:
defects breed individuality. Brokenness

is random, internal, seldom mirrored by appearance.
You can't presume to suffer it, but in your mind of Spring
you know it as a prelude to rebirth.

Hopper Street, Bendigo

Crisp with frost at dawn, streets of crushed quartzite dazzle by noon. We walk to the Station, peer for hours between wrought footbridge slats. A man crawls the train rooves, their full length, drops chunks of ice into circular lidded holes. A visiting evangelist talks about the Lord: now and then someone gives their life to Him. Down the street, a man is giving up the bottle; his children have received decent clothes. All the untainted days, coruscating light, the words: antimacassar, aspidistra, epergne. A pulley-lift from the cellar; long-handled iron pots on a wood stove; creamy porridge, gentle lumpiness, sugar as dark as the mission field. At Hermannsburg, they're grateful for each knitted item, are learning to write.

Parting driveway gravel after a downpour, grandpa's stick scratches for gold specks. He wears a three-piece suit all summer, even on wildflower trips to The Whipstick or teaching us to catch yabbies. He remembers the first car in Bendigo, a man walking ahead to ease the alarm of horses. At the sheep sales ("Been a bit dry." "Mmm, a bit dry.") grandma stays in the car, reads *Tidings.* Strong believers these, the opposite of insouciant. Actually friendly: no hidden-agenda smile, no evangel-blight. We're less sinners than forgetters, says grandpa, leather armchaired, lead-lighted. In the Buick, we take food cartons to miners' families. Central Deborah is shutting down.

4 Poems

1. The Old School, Macquarie Street

I spend a year of lunch-times
locked in a lavatory.
Each day at noon
I shove the bolt across.

On a warm, wooden seat
below a cast-iron cistern,
I write letters to God.

The floor conjures a fantasy
of blue-tongue lizards, greenhood orchids.
They creep out of cavities,
push through cement.

2. Sundays

Boys of our type grew up slowly
in the plane-tree suburbs,
believing Gelatine came
from bread-cart horses' powdered hooves,

and hair on women's bodies
in the National Gallery
was shadow.

Belief had hop-scotched
free of doubt. God wanted
our attendance, two sessions
each Sunday.
                    The chaplain said

if everyone accepted Jesus
there would be no more cruelty
to pigeons.

We had found pigeons' legs
scattered in the playground –
snipped off with scissors,
casually arranged like cake forks.

3. Army Cadet Camp, Brighton

We stood naked in the drill hall,
a circle of slate-cold waifs
clutching breath.
A medical team right-wheeled
from boy to boy; three officers
stood at the edge,
arms folded, eyes darting.
We dressed and fled,
or sauntered out. A gang
of older boys would grab a younger boy,
drag him to a dormitory,
finish the examination.

4. Boarding House

"Under the door of the next room
is an uncommonly wide strip of light.
Get down on your knees and bend forward
until your head touches the floor.
Turn your head to one side and creep
sideways until your lower eye is up against
the strip. If the deputy house master
encompasses the assistant cook, report back."

Minnie and Jacko

Minnie's name is a derivation of Miniature, a title used by everyone to distinguish him from Jacko, his brother. Minnie is shorter and slighter than me, but stronger. I walk up to his front door, usually with a comic (borrowed from under my brother's bed) to ensure access to Minnie's Dinky Toys and forbidden cowboy weaponry: tin-plated pistols, rifles, sling-shots. Well, I walk to the door and Minnie springs at me, flattens me on the buffalo grass, screams in Apache, or similar, a language I guess he's picked up from movies. He grabs the sides of my head, beats it into the turf until his Nanna, in blue-spotted apron, comes out – likewise screaming – bidding him desist.

Our clubhouse, a corner section of Minnie's filled-in back verandah, bares the motto: "Reasons For Everything." Our purpose is to award ourselves badges. We cut triangles from an old sheet and write on them with biro: "For Fairness." "For Not Fighting." In the middle of the clubhouse table is a glass jar containing a human poo. The poo is from Jacko, who dropped it delicately into a screw-top jar when he heard that Minnie and I were looking for something special around which to base our deliberations. Jacko's gift is well-received by members, but because he's a Scout we don't let him join. Since my parents deny me permission to become so much as a Cub, I argue that Jacko be debarred or the club disband. Devastated, Jacko threatens to leave home and become a tent pegger with Worth's Circus. We commonly talk of being tent peggers: you travel to every city and see naked women close-up.

Cassowary

With an axe-head for a hat,

blue neck with red scarf

and skirt tugged shyly

over knee-rind,

she charges through jungle

with outstretched plumage,

her blade fending off

tendrils of liana

or draped cables

of strangler fig.

Wandering,

she scuffs humus,

steals bananas.

Her cough,

like a rivet into galvo.

The Vital Ignorance

It's all very well for those with faith,
my friend remarks, dismissive and stark,
as if faith were something other
than incentive to explore the dark.

New Norcia Boys

1849

Two Aboriginal boys are ushered into the Vatican,
by guards holding spears which are far too thick.
They kneel, and kiss the ring of Pius IX.

But Francis Conaci and John Dirimera,
of the tribe Nyungar, are not flummoxed.
From childhood they have seen the sacredness

of people,
and having, after a fashion,
seen God,

no Pope can daunt them.
Neither can a shelter built of stone
perplex them, nor priests

who prop themselves
in carved trees,
and talk to everyone without listening.

Only this unsettles the boys:
the sight of elders curiously uncared for
on the portico steps, and water everywhere
unfit to drink.

*

"These dear boys, Holy Father,"
(begins Dom Rosendo Salvado)
"will take the Word of Truth

to their tar-brushed brethren, the Australians."
Dirimera recites a phrase learnt on the voyage:
Venite, ambulemus in Lumine, let us walk in the light,

to which the Pope appends an elegant reply.
Salvado continues his report: "The tribe of Australians,
who call themselves *Nyungar,* are not devoid

of God's revelation. Their ingenious
culture is cleverly adapted to harsh conditions.
They have no chiefs, no police, no law courts

and no prisons. Their system of land tenure,
their ceremonies and traditions, are recorded only
in the tribal mind. Theirs is a deep, inner

listening, a patient means of touching mystery.
Through living with the Nyungar, I am persuaded
of the need to protect these courteous
people from the colonists who covet their land."

*

Watching with long, long thoughts,
Conaci and Dirimera understand the tenor
of the words. At home, they would've sung
what couldn't be said.

Sicily: their host is a prelate who can't decide
which wines to do without for Lent.
Floating beef fat, on his plate,
reflects the purple road map on his nose.
He talks of lower standards, weaker links.
Knowing otherwise,
they hear his easy answers fall like tassels

from the hems of holy gowns.
Men in copes or chasubles don't disconcert them,
nor Sicilian royalty. Not aspiring to status,
they have never thought to compare themselves
with others.

*

1851

The boys are weary of laying out
vestments, filling incense boats,
and setting credence tables before Mass.

The Benedictine habit proves more comfortable
than trousers. Swirling along one afternoon
to San Giovanni in Laterano,

the boys practice their Latin
in the vast coldness
and ask if they can light and swing a thurible.

"Yes, why not?" says the sacristan,
and they whir it about their heads
in a rear cloister, laughing.

*

1853

Sleep closes the eyes of Conaci upon a prayer.
His mind has descended to his heart
and is held there.
In the morning,
he doesn't wake.

Salvado writes to Bishop Brady, in Perth:
"Our young brother Francis has died in Rome,
far from the comfort of his people.
My sadness is tempered
by joy that the boy embodied our Saviour,
and showed the holy and the ordinary to be equal.
... I continue to recruit men for New Norcia."

*

1855

At shouts of land,
Dirimera crawls back on deck.
He props himself against the rudder-case
to scan the coast.

Sailors carry him ashore at Fremantle.

Nyungar elders are summoned by the Bishop:
"I would have you arrive with all haste.
He is tubercular, gravely ill."

The elders nourish Dirimera with fruit mash,
array him in currajong leaves, chant him
toward death. They satisfy themselves:
he has remembered just enough.

On a branch, a bronzewing pigeon bobs,
bobs its head. A faint breeze splays
the slighter feathers,
reveals a glint
of copper,
emerald.

The Solitary

If you visit the Mani,
which hangs like a satyr's leg
from the Peloponnese,
you might board a little boat
at Mezalimonas, and journey south.

If you keep close to the cliffs,
you might see a hole,
high in the cliff-face.

A monk's cell,
hewn in the rock;
a mansion for unseen presences,
where sea-birds cry their response
to versicles.

On days of flat calm,
fishermen have heard a steady clink
of chisel on stone:
the monk, chipping his tomb.

Breathing Boulder

I once knew a woman
who collected fragments
from French cathedral walls.

She claimed they cleaned the air,
which she could hear,
glistening,
on windless nights.

Sensing a subtle joy,
I called her *Balmy*,
although her carbuncular skin
was anything but placid.

Each morning, she liberated moths
trapped behind glass,
picked up earthworms
before they steamed to pretzels
on the path, shook ants from cut gladioli.

Balmy took me bushwalking
to see a certain boulder:
lichen-spotted, bull-shouldered.

I looked until I saw,
or thought I saw,
an infinitesimal
rise and fall:

igneous passion in motion,
stabilised for an aeon

and now stilled,
                        or perhaps not.
I felt part of a backdrop
of presence,
as if all things participated
in a gossamered influence,
a cloud of utterance.

Do you see

my paper

boat

of spiritual ambition

bob once,

twice,

then fall apart

in the torrent?

Aye, there be no ice

Wandering the coast of northern Donegal, toward a western valley favoured by Colum Cille. Soft rain changes to a dry, cold wind. I stop at Andara, to hear that ice and snow is clear of Glenesh Pass. There'll be no need to take the longer, safer route. "Aye, 'tis a good road through the Glenesh," says a volunteer at the advice desk. "Aye, there be no ice. No ice on account of the wind." Later, the car is sliding sideways, down the slope I've just come up.

In Colum Cille's glen, I drive slowly, looking for somewhere to stay. An old man opens his door, looks at me. I wind the window down. He calls: "Is that you Kevin?" "No." "It's not you, Kevin?" "Sorry, no." Inside his cottage, by a fire of two turfs, we talk over tea and soda bread. He shows me a photo of his nephew Kevin, who lives in Sydney. "Do you know Kevin?" "No." "Ye don't live at Sydney?" "Sorry, no." But Kevin isn't really expected, and perhaps has no plans to travel. "I heard a car. And I looked out. And I thought, it could be Kevin. If he came to visit, it would be in a car. St Colum Cille came to see the stones here. Ye know about the birds, the injured birds. St Colum Cille kept many birds. Ye know that through the prayers of St Brigit, I haven't touched the drink since June the eleventh, 1987."

He gives me a St Brigit's Cross, woven last February from reeds. The faintly green arms, equal in length, are neatly secured with tape. Insisting on coming out to the car, he puts the cross behind the sun visor on the passenger side. "Aye, through the prayers of St Brigit, no real harm will come ye."

Sister Spider

This large, sedentary spider
which shares our bathroom,

spending hours wiping droplets
from her leg hair,

has a dusting of animated poppy seeds
on her back.

Greetings, spiders, with whom we inhabit
common space;

and potoroo and magpie, also having a part
in us, and we with you.

Greetings to everyday epiphanies;
not forgetting you insects,

in bodiliness our brothers;
and you, the unseen forms

which might infect, or assist,
being heirs with us and all the other creatures

which walk, crawl, fly, slide, multiply,
divide or stay put;

joint heirs of such molecular inheritance
that where our skin stops,

our bodies do not stop,
greetings.

Notes

Tinderbox Hills: south of Hobart, a modest hilly ridge overlooking the River Derwent's mouth to the east and Bruny Island to the south.

Koonya: no woman of this actual name is known to have lived on Bass Strait's Furneaux Group, of which Cape Barren Island forms a part.

To Governor George Arthur In Heaven: Lieutenant Governor of Van Diemen's Land from 1823 to1837, Arthur was under New South Wales jurisdiction and answerable to the Home Office at Westminster. Lines 17 and 18 reflect the version of Matthew 5:37 with which Arthur was familiar.

Convict Brick: a small village (Koonya: *black swan*) grew up around these barracks on Tasman Peninsula, Van Diemen's Land (not officially 'Tasmania' until 1855).

Truganini's Soliloquy: Truganini died in Hobart in 1876.

Cousin Gwen: the biscuit plate text is drawn from Revelation 21:4 & 5.

Possum: the green hue of the Green Ringtail (restricted in range to parts of far north-east Queensland) is the combined effect of its grey, white and yellow pigmented hair.

Father Kolbe: Maximilian Kolbe volunteered to die in the place of Franciszek Gajowniczek, who survived Auschwitz, was reunited with his wife, and died in his native Poland in 1995, aged 93. He did not again see their two children, both of whom died under bombardment in Poland in January 1945.

Cassowary: technically a ratite, and not a bird, the southern or double-wattled cassowary is thought to be an ancestor of the lighter, taller, and much more common emu.

New Norcia Boys: Salvado and his fellow Benedictine, Joseph Serra, co-founded the Monastery of New Norcia, north of Perth, in 1846.